CLOTHING, COSTUMES, and UNIFORMS
Throughout
AMERICAN HISTORY™

What People Wore
On
Southern Plantations

∞ Allison Stark Draper ∞

The Rosen Publishing Group's
PowerKids Press™
New York

For my mother

Published in 2001 by The Rosen Publishing Group, Inc.
29 East 21st Street, New York, NY 10010

First Edition

Book Design: Emily Muschinske

Photo Credits: pp. 3, 17 (man) © Mercury Archives/Image Bank; pp. 4, 11,12, 13, 14, 15 (fan), 16, 22 © Jeffrey Foxx; p. 5 (plantation house and cotton plant) © Robert Holmes/CORBIS; pp. 5 (slave quarters), 8 © Civil War Foundation; pp. 6, 15 (bonnet), 17 (top hat), 20 © Emily Muschinske; pp. 7, 18, 21 © North Wind Pictures; p. 9 © American Stock/Archive Photos; p. 15 (woman) © Bettmann/CORBIS; p. 19 © William A. Blake/CORBIS.

Draper, Allison Stark.
    What people wore on southern plantations / Allison Stark Draper.
      p. cm.— (Clothing, costumes, and uniforms throughout American history)
    Includes index.
    Summary: This book describes what people wore on Southern plantations, discussing the clothes of the wealthy plantation owners, the hoop skirts worn by the Southern women in the 1800s, and the clothes made on the plantation for the slaves.
    ISBN 0-8239-5668-7
    1. Costume—Southern states—History—Juvenile literature. 2. Plantation life—Southern states—History—Juvenile literature. 3. Southern states—Social life and customs—Juvenile literature. [1. Costume—History. 2. Plantation life. 3. Southern states—Social life and customs.] I. Title. II. Series.

GT617.S59 D73 2000
391'.00975—dc21   00-033993

Manufactured in the United States of America

Contents

The Rise of Southern Plantations

In 1607, the first **settlers** came to America from England. They settled in a **colony** in Jamestown, Virginia. These early Virginians grew tobacco on large farms called plantations. By the mid-1600s, most plantation owners used slaves **kidnapped** from Africa to work in their fields. The **cruel** practice of slavery lasted over 200 years. Slaves were not paid and had no freedom.

By the late 1700s, cotton was the crop most often grown on plantations. The plantation way of life lasted until the 1860s. The owners became rich by selling their crops. They showed off their wealth by wearing fancy clothes made from fine fabrics that they bought in England.

A cotton hat called a mobcap protected girls and women from the heat of the sun.

The houses where slaves lived were very small, unlike the homes of plantation owners and their families. These fancy homes, called mansions, might have up to 30 bedrooms.

Clothes of the Early Plantation Owners

The plantation owners of the 1600s copied the clothing styles of wealthy men in England. The clothes were made of fine cloth such as velvet or silk. Plantation owners wore short, close-fitting jackets called doublets. They slashed the sleeves of the doublets to show off the brightly colored shirts they wore underneath. They also wore padded pants called **breeches** that came down to their knees. Men wore silk stockings and shoes with high heels. They wore hats with feathers. These feathers were held in place with precious stones and gems. When the weather became cold, plantation owners carried fur **muffs** to keep their hands warm.

Early plantation owners wore short, fitted jackets called doublets.

These wealthy plantation owners are wearing clothes made from costly fabric such as silk or velvet. They are also wearing breeches, doublets, and hats with long feathers on them.

Field Slaves and House Slaves

When slavery first began in the mid-1600s, there were slaves in both the North and South. In time many Northerners came to believe that slavery was cruel and should be illegal. It was also easier for Northern farmers to do without slaves. Farms were  smaller and could be run by the farmer and his family. Crops raised in the South required a lot of workers, however, so the **brutal** practice of slavery remained a part of plantation life until the end of the **Civil War**. While most slaves were forced to work in the fields, some slaves worked inside the plantation owner's house. These people were

Female house slaves wore lightweight dresses to try to keep them cool as they did their chores for the plantation owner and his family.

Field slaves worked long hours picking cotton. They wore cotton clothes and hats or scarves to try to stay cool.

called house slaves. Male slaves who worked in the fields were given a hat, shirt, and breeches to wear. Female field slaves wore simple cotton dresses. Sometimes the field slaves were also given stockings and a pair of shoes. House slaves were sometimes dressed in uniforms that used the family colors as trim.

A Plantation Lady

By the late 1700s, American colonists decided that they wanted their **independence** from England. The English did not want to give up control of the colonies. This led to the **Revolutionary War**. While Southern men fought in the war, women ran the plantations. They learned how to make their own thread, yarn, and cloth. They also made uniforms for the army. The Americans won the war in 1783. The **antebellum** period was the time between the Revolutionary War and the Civil War. During this period, changes in clothing styles often started in the North. Southern women had to wait to hear of new styles. One dress worn during this time was the Promenade dress. This dress had a long waist and wide sleeves. It was made of a shiny, woven fabric called taffeta, or other fine cloth.

This woman is dressed like a nineteenth century woman. She is wearing a bell-shaped dress with a separate lace collar. The collar could be taken off and washed without washing the whole dress.

Plantation women wore hair nets to keep their hair out of the way while they worked in the house.

Women wore straw hats. They changed the band around the hat to give it a different look.

This bag is made from fabric and is pulled closed using a drawstring.

The Hoop Skirt

In the 1800s, women on southern plantations began wearing hoop skirts. These skirts had a stiff, round hoop sewn into them. The hoop was worn under a woman's dress. It made the bottom part of the dress wide, but not heavy. Dresses were pulled in tightly around the waist, and then they widened around the floor. At this time, it was thought to be a sign of beauty to have a small waist. Women wore **corsets** to make their waists as small as possible. The corsets were made with whalebone or steel and were closed in the front and tied in the back. Corsets were tied so tight that sometimes women fainted. They carried **smelling salts** to wake them up if they fainted from wearing a tight corset.

Women wore belts to draw attention to their small waists.

The women in these photographs are dressed like nineteenth century women. Plantation women would wear up to six layers of undergarments, called petticoats, to make their skirts look full.

Girls and women wore garments called bloomers under their clothes.

Hoops gave dresses the bell-like shape that was popular during the 1800s.

Staying out of the Sun

In the antebellum South, pale skin was a sign of beauty, so the plantation owners' wives tried to stay out of the sun. They wore cotton hats called sunbonnets to protect their faces when they were outside. Sunbonnets had wide brims that protected the face. They usually had a ruffle in the back to protect the neck from the sun. Plantation ladies also wore leather or silk gloves to protect their hands. Parasols were small umbrellas that women used to protect themselves

Hats had wide brims to protect women from the heat and keep their skin pale. They decorated the hats with flowers and ribbons.

Ladies often wore white gloves to protect their hands from the sun and from dirt.

14

from the sun. Some parasols were made of silk with a wooden handle and a small hook. On hot days, women carried hand fans to keep cool. The fans had beautiful designs on them.

A sunbonnet protected a woman's face from the sun.

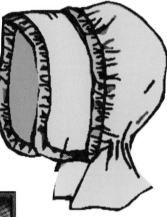

Parasols shaded women from the sun. They were made from fancy fabrics and had a hook at the end to help women carry them.

Some fans had perfume on them to freshen the air when a woman fanned herself.

Trousers and Top Hats

In the mid-1800s, men began wearing long pants called trousers instead of breeches. They stopped wearing stockings and wore short socks. Wealthy plantation owners bought much of their clothing from Europe. They also had clothes made for them by tailors. These men wore waistcoats, or vests, made out of rich fabric such as silk or velvet. The waistcoats were fastened with jeweled buttons and buckles. Under the waistcoat, plantation owners wore white shirts made out of fine cloth. They wore high boots made of black leather. These boots were called Wellington boots.

This Southern man is wearing a vest with a "V" shaped collar.

Men wore silk or fur hats called top hats.

16

Men also wore tall hats called top hats. Top hats were made out of silk or fur. Most top hats were black, but gray and white were also popular colors.

Making Clothes and Quilts

Plantation owners' wives would knit and sew for their families. They had house slaves to help them. The plantation owner's wife had a large household. She had to make sure that her husband, children, and slaves had clothing for the year. Young girls were taught to sew by making samplers. Samplers were small pieces of fabric that usually had letters or sayings sewn into them. Mothers gave their older, unmarried daughters the job of making the slaves' clothes. Unmarried daughters who worked on the spinning wheel were called "spinsters." Women made stockings and undergarments for themselves. They also made linen and quilts. A quilt is a bed covering filled with material or feathers and covered by scraps of leftover material in a pretty design.

18

This woman is sewing a quilt.

Quilts are made by sewing together different pieces of cloth. This is a good way of using extra bits of cloth left over from other material.

Children on the Plantation

The plantation owner's sons and daughters wore dresses until they were five or six years old. The dresses were a long shirt with strings attached to the back. The strings were used to guide children when they learned to walk. Sometimes boys wore suits called skeleton suits. These were shirts and pants that buttoned together at the waist. When boys turned six they were "breeched." This meant that they wore breeches like their fathers.

As girls grew, they wore corsets and dresses like their mothers. Their dresses had a full skirt and tight **bodice**. The plantation owner's children were expected to act and dress like little adults.

Girls wore aprons called pinafores to keep their dresses clean. The pinafore could be made longer and wider as the girl grew.

Wealthy plantation children dressed like adults once they turned five or six.

Southern Soldiers' Uniforms

By the mid-1800s, the Northern and Southern states were divided about slavery. Northerners thought slavery was so unfair that it had to stop. Southerners wanted to keep their slaves to avoid paying workers. When the North and South could not agree, the Civil War began in 1861. Southern soldiers wore wool uniforms. Most of the uniforms were gray, but they also wore blue pants, gray frock coats, and dark caps. Southern soldiers could not always get uniforms. Many had to wear their own clothes that they dyed gray. The Civil War ended in 1865. The Thirteenth **Amendment** to the **Constitution**, which ended slavery, was made a law the same year. The age of the Southern plantation had lasted over 200 years. Now it was coming to an end.

This man dressed like a Southern soldier. He is wearing a waist-length jacket called a "shell" jacket. The close-up of his button has an "I" on it. This stands for "infantry," the foot soldiers of the Southern army.

Glossary

amendment (ah-MEND-ment) An addition or change to the Constitution.

antebellum (an-tih-BEH-lem) The time in American history between the Revolutionary War and the Civil War. In Latin, antebellum means "before the war."

bodice (BOD-is) The upper part of a woman's dress.

breeches (BREE-chez) Pants that come down to a man's calves.

brutal (BRU-tul) Harsh, unfeeling, inhumane.

Civil War (SIH-vul WOR) The war fought between the Northern and Southern states from 1861 to 1865.

colony (KAH-luh-nee) An area in a new country where a large group of people live that are still ruled by the leaders and laws of their old country.

Constitution (KAHN-stih-TOO-shun) The set of rules by which the United States is governed.

corsets (KOR-sitz) Undergarments worn around the middle of the body that are tightened with laces.

cruel (KROOL) Very mean.

independence (in-dih-PEN-dents) Freedom from the control, support, or help of other people.

kidnapped (KID-napt) Carried off by force.

muffs (MUFS) Coverings of fur or other material for keeping both hands warm.

Revolutionary War (REH-vuh-LOO-shun-nayr-ee WOR) The war that American colonists fought from 1775 to 1781 to win independence from England.

settlers (SEHT-lerz) People who move to a new land to live.

smelling salts (SMEL-ing SALTS) Strong-smelling chemicals that can wake a person when he or she faints.

Index

Web Sites

To learn more about what people wore on Southern Plantations, check out this Web site:

http://www.monticello.org/plantation/textile.html